Praise for

When No Thing Works

"This slender volume is a bountiful exhortation of the human spirit's potential to unwind intractable challenges of our 'collective acceleration,' and a sharp knife that slices through wishful, lazy, or destructive machinations to get there.

Wong Rōshi's unique confluence of locations, lineages, and experience are honed into a wisdom lens we can peer through to couple our Why and our Way. Like all great teachers, she imparts story and strategy with equal measures of humility, reminding us that how we *be* matters to how we *become*.

Lyrical, sure, and threaded with the deft insight and forgiving humor of a guide who knows how flawed we can be, Wong Rōshi offers not so much a map, but a strategic pointing to the constellation of choices and practices we can and must navigate to enter a slipstream into an ever-possible future, together.

This work is a triumph, and you can feel the thunderous dance of ancestors'—past and future—approval."

> —REV. ANGEL KYODO WILLIAMS, Rōshi, coauthor
> of *Radical Dharma*

"Norma Wong has been a compelling teacher in the realm of transformation for years—when I met her she was somehow one with the floor as several grownups tried with zero success to lift her up. I wanted to learn everything about that grounding. In this tight, engaging work, Norma is walking us through current events and possibilities, pointing out the actual currents, the questions, the timeplaces and emergent worldviews that most matter. This is deep, no-nonsense grounding, taught lightly, with invitation and humor and curiosity. Profound and embodied in each line . . . I know I will return to this text over and over. I join Norma on the path toward 'interdependent thriving,' toward a visionary spacetime that grows from the seeds of our practice in the here and now."

—ADRIENNE MAREE BROWN, author of *Emergent Strategy*

"Norma Ryuko Kawelokū Wong explores the essence of a twenty-first-century Indigenous worldview in *When No Thing Works*. She relies on knowing that all things, past and future, are in relationship. What we imagine and how we walk in the present determines the future. As Norma signals, our walk must include leaps that take us into unknowns, but we will not be alone. Norma gives us wise counsel for this difficult moment on Mother Earth. One culture, one belief system, one community alone is unable to fulfill our ancestors' collective hopes for all of our descendants. As Norma's ancestors said, 'O ka ehu kakahiaka . . . The red dawn of our people became the red dawn of many peoples.' Hawwih (thank you in Caddo), Norma, your family, and your people!"

—JUDITH LEBLANC, citizen of the Caddo Nation, ekah (grandmother), and executive director of the Native Organizers Alliance

"This is no ordinary book—it is more of a koan, a dreamspace poem, a love letter to future descendants. It lives at the intersections of reflective political analysis about the pivotal, cleaving moment we are currently experiencing and future stories of 'the world as we would have it be.' With an expansive understanding of emergent worldview, strategy and practice, the author weaves a web of mutuality that inspires a more interconnected version of the future and ourselves."

—TESSA HICKS PETERSON, associate professor of urban studies and coauthor of *Practicing Liberation*

"As we stand at the threshold of collapsing systems and broken hearts, there is an opening. In *When No Thing Works*, Rōshi Norma Wong gives us a compass for how to navigate the space in between where we are coming from and where we are going. This book is an invitation to practice who we need to be to meet this moment and shape a future of possibility and potential."

—KERRI KELLY, author of *American Detox*

"So many colleagues and friends have benefited from the teachings of Norma Wong—and now more of us can see why. In a time in which our movements are grappling with the balance between soul and strategy—between the bonding warmth of mutual connection and the steely strength of political solidarity—this book lands as both a provocation and an invitation. It forces you to think, encourages you to feel, and slows you down enough to realize that the urgency of now must be tempered by a sense of timeless purpose. Breathe deep—another world is indeed possible if we dream, align, and act."

—MANUEL PASTOR, distinguished professor of sociology, American studies, and ethnicity at USC

"My copy of this book will have its pages with corners worn, its margins filled with scribbled notes, and its passages highlighted in different colors. Every time I pick up this book, I will have countless 'aha' moments. How do I know? From years of studying with Norma. From years of taking notes from Norma's talks. From years of looking back at my notes and seeing the words that I need to see in that moment. In the words of Anaïs Nin, 'We don't see things as they are; we see them as we are.' We see Norma's words as we are. As we are ready. As we arise."

—JENNIFER ITO, research director at USC Equity Research Institute

"Navigating us with ease and grace, *When No Thing Works* is a compelling narrative on how we might actually get it right if we align our actions with what these times require of us. From re-humanizing and healing ourselves and our communities to shifting habits that no longer serve us, Norma Wong reminds us that a future of mutual stewardship and thriving for all living things is possible. Deeply aware of the complex systems accelerating before us all, she outlines hopeful actions: breathing deeply and slowly, seeing and defining our collective purpose, and making clear choices that reveal our interdependence as a core value. These are just glimpses of the deeply wise guidance that Wong Rōshi beautifully articulates. This is a book I will return to often for the many insights that live throughout this clear and delightful expression of aloha."

—PAM OMIDYAR, cofounder of the Omidyar Group

"Are you committed to a just and beautiful world and community, but find yourself losing hope and feeling overwhelmed? This is a timely book for navigating the convergence of crises, increasing division, and times of shift that we find ourselves in as a human family. Norma Wong deftly weaves Zen wisdom, Indigenous teachings, gifted storytelling, nature patterns, quantum physics, poetry, sharp analysis, strategy, and practice to help us understand how we can create a different way forward. Her book reminds us that our choices, actions, relationships, and practices in this time have the power to create and shape the future, not only for ourselves, but for the Earth and for the next seven generations. This book is an emergent call to action for our times, to practice and imagine, to arise together, and energetically draw a different future and worldview to us."

—BRENDA SALGADO, speaker, spiritual teacher, curandera, toltec energy healer, and author of *Real World Mindfulness for Beginners*

"*When No Thing Works* defies literary categorization. It is speculative nonfiction. It is historical current events. It is the math of science + spirit + imagination. It is humanities (as in humanity plural). Every page contains a focal point for future-casting. Whether you read the pages in order, or wander randomly through the chapters, the learning and wonder will remain constant. Collectively—as readers, students, and friends all—we can, indeed we must, animate the text. Life on Earth requires nothing less."

—NAN STOOPS, former director and strategic advisor for the Washington State Coalition Against Domestic Violence

"Having had the honor of learning from Norma Wong over the past several years as a student of her movement-building work, reading the book was like sitting in the room listening to her tell stories filled with wisdom and humor that always bring levity during a time that often feels so heavy. She has somehow captured the spirit of hope in this timeplace of collapse, and has encouraged us to go beyond the current frames of our worldview and enter into a worldview of emergence and interdependence. Norma has written us a book of brilliant strategy illustrated through beautiful stories told in a way only a Zen master could do. She has gifted us a treasure map on how to leap toward the horizon and cocreate the world we are reimagining for the descendants of our descendants. We are excited to integrate this book into our work at the Beloved Communities Network. As we work to embody the vision of transitioning to a world of love, resilience, and regeneration, this book unlocks the simple truth that it will require both consciousness action and the sharp discipline of choice."

—LEILA MCCABE, director of the Beloved Communities Network

"If you want to understand how things can come together, you have to honor and understand the ways and the why of how they are falling apart. When 'nothing works,' it can help us to pivot and return to deeper ancestral understandings of what 'working' truly is. Who are we and why are we here? What is the meaning of our existence, connection, and creativity? What are our sacred responsibilities to our ancestors, future generations, and all living beings? Kawelokū's book invites us into the practice of these questions. And in living through these questions together, 'a way forward' emerges out of our collective practice of love and care. Out of many ways and from many people, Norma shines light on a way forward together that is only possible if each of us bring all of who we are, wholeheartedly, to each step, each breath, and each bold act of collective courage and action. Rōshi Norma is helping us to create the path by walking it together with us."

—TAJ JAMES, founder of the Movement Strategy Center and Full Spectrum Capital

"Hand-wringing, hair-pulling, growing anxiety, trepidation, polarization, and despair are all too common and personally familiar responses to the current state of the world around us. It is tempting to become caught up in these collective responses and there are even times when it seems like there is no path available to a more hopeful future. *When No Thing Works*, however, beautifully and courageously lays out a path for the ready, willing, and open to choose another way.

For those of us who will dare to believe in the collective potential of our humanity and who choose to evolve, to imagine, to leap toward the unknown together, this book is the gift of a roadmap that we can begin to follow today. Here Norma Ryūkō Kawelokū Wong Rōshi combines

and documents, with clarity and simplicity, the wisdom she has cultivated through deep cultural rootedness, applied Zen, and strategy in
one place—a compelling invitation into what we can do, even in these
troubling times, to create the lasting, transformative impact made
possible with others driven by big purpose. Get ready to reconnect to
hopefulness about what is possible, not by wishing on the stars, but by
realizing the potential within us all, together, to be the stuff of starlight
to a decaying world that, more than ever, needs us to be awake and take
big leaps toward a horizon in which our descendants and our planet
thrive."

—ALEXIS FLANAGAN, coexecutive director of the Resonance
Network

"This is a must-read infused with invitation to (re)imagine our future
selves sipping tea in order to dream at rhythms that defy description.
When our descendents come across this book in a library, they will sip
tea made with clean water, weave stories of wholeness and kuleana while
reminding themselves to continue to water the soil of storytelling as they
too have learned from us the power of the critical juncture.

This book invites the warrior poet in us. It deftly asks us to dream
even as we question our worthiness. Norma infuses humor amidst
the brackish waters of our realities while imploring us to lean into
what 'reflective discernment' means to us, but to do that discerning
across two-leggeds, four-leggeds, wingeds and more; across centuries
of humanity with integrity and love. This means we need to clear our
decks, breathe deeply, and dream into being a newer fruitful emergence
of interdependent thriving.

Norma's book weaves a path for us to leap, aim, and act at a rhythm
that is invited by the Earth's drumbeat. The prosiest of phrases and
more lyrical of verses ask us to examine the devastating landscapes, but
more importantly remind us that our habits unexamined can and will
be the end of us—and by *us* she means humanity, not individualism.
She invites us to a deeper practice than we have ever attempted. And
she is right."

—DR. SHADIIN GARCIA, cohost of the *Dive-In Justice* podcast
and principal of Shoreline Consulting

When
No
Thing
Works

When No Thing Works

A Zen and Indigenous Perspective on Resilience, Shared Purpose, and Leadership in the Timeplace of Collapse

Norma Ryūkō Kawelokū Wong Rōshi

North Atlantic Books
Huichin, unceded Ohlone land
Berkeley, California

North Atlantic Books
Huichin, unceded Ohlone land
2526 Martin Luther King Jr Way
Berkeley, CA 94704 USA
www.northatlanticbooks.com

Cover art © panimoni via Getty Images
Cover design by Jess Morphew
Book design by Happenstance Type-O-Rama
Printed in Canada

When No Thing Works: A Zen and Indigenous Perspective on Resilience, Shared Purpose, and Leadership in the Timeplace of Collapse is sponsored and published by North Atlantic Books, an educational nonprofit based in the unceded Ohlone land Huichin (Berkeley, CA) that collaborates with partners to develop cross-cultural perspectives; nurture holistic views of art, science, the humanities, and healing; and seed personal and global transformation by publishing work on the relationship of body, spirit, and nature.

North Atlantic Books's publications are distributed to the US trade and internationally by Penguin Random House Publisher Services. For further information, visit our website at www.northatlanticbooks.com.

The authorized representative in the EU for product safety and compliance is Eucomply OÜ, Pärnu mnt 139b-14, 11317 Tallinn, Estonia, hello@eucompliancepartner.com, +33757690241.

Library of Congress Cataloging-in-Publication Data
Names: Wong, Norma Ryūkō Kawelokū, 1956- author.
Title: When no thing works : a Zen and indigenous perspective on resilience, shared purpose, and leadership in the timeplace of collapse / Norma Ryūkō Kawelokū Wong.
Description: Berkeley, California : North Atlantic Books, [2024] | Includes bibliographical references. | Summary: "Spiritual and community lessons for embracing collective care, co-creating sustainable futures, and responsibly meeting uncertain futures-a Zen and Native Hawaiian take on building better, more balanced ways of being"-- Provided by publisher.
Identifiers: LCCN 2024003166 (print) | LCCN 2024003167 (ebook) | ISBN 9798889840992 (paperback) | ISBN 9798889841005 (epub)
Subjects: LCSH: Resilience (Personality trait) | Sustainability. | Leadership.
Classification: LCC BF698.35.R47 W65 2024 (print) | LCC BF698.35.R47 (ebook) | DDC 650.1--dc23/eng/20240511
LC record available at https://lccn.loc.gov/2024003166
LC ebook record available at https://lccn.loc.gov/2024003167

The interior of this book is printed on 100 percent recycled paper, and the cover is printed on material from well-managed forests.

4 5 6 7 8 9 FRIESENS 28 27 26 25

Acknowledgments

With much aloha I humbly acknowledge ancestors all, teachers many, students who are my teachers, family of course—especially my sister who is my housemate, colleagues who are friends, fellow warriors, fellow priests, generals bar none, descendants not yet born, songs, stories, chants, the islands of my birthplace, ancient places beyond the horizon, the valley that is my home, the great oceans uniting us, the winds that speak, the life-giving water . . . mahalo nui loa, so much gratitude.

Contents

Foreword

By
Nā'ālehu Anthony

It certainly feels like the world has sped up in recent years. I can't put my finger on the moment when it occurred, but with news breaking minute by minute and global crisis after global crisis occurring seemingly every week, it's hard for some of us to get to a place of sitting and thinking about topics that are not hinged on the *now*. Indeed, our whole world may be collectively accelerating.

I've had the privilege of spending time on the road and back at home in Hawai'i with Norma for about a decade and a half. With Norma, I have sat in rooms at home in Hawai'i and across the continent, where people committed to the repair of the long arc—activists, visionaries, movement people—continue to come and seek her counsel. When I look back at those experiences, being invited in the room with her and others, like me, who are trying to make sense of this speeding-up world, I have a growing appreciation of two things that have become clearer as I have learned at her side.

The first is that Norma has the ability to slow things down for her students, or those she is spending time with, while we are in a shared space. Even though sometimes it feels like the days are still moving quickly, and some of the content discussed is still ripped from the headlines of the latest news feeds, we are able to digest these events in different and more interconnected ways. These are the few days that I can feel really grounded, when there is time to reset. This different rhythm for time and space has a profound effect on what kind of discussion we have and how we can have it.

The second is that the conversations anchored by Norma's perspectives and frameworks really allow for a broader view of what's happening in the now. While the next election or the next crisis certainly has a net effect on our daily lives, there is also a conversation to have as we plan and look farther out into the unknown—past the horizon that we can see. These times in discussion buoy many of us into a context of what really matters and how we can reframe the now more usefully. Pursuing a farther horizon really matters as we move faster, for not just us in the now but for those yet to come.

It is with this explanation of what can happen "in the room" with which I hope you can hold this book. Many of us have been urging Norma to write to a broader audience. Yes, she has written many things and used them as tools in these teachings. Yes, she wrote many, many important pieces in her previous life in her policy career. But what we have been urging her to do is to step out of the here and now and "in the room" herself and write something that can take many more of us on a journey at the critical time to look past the limits of what we thought we could see.

To be clear, I don't think it was our urging that produced this piece; I think it was the time of this collective acceleration the world is in that brought her to an understanding that something must be done to help people understand what's happening. She does this with poetic ease. She somehow dropped the barrier to her stream of consciousness and let all of us in. In this text, we sit next to her as she grapples with these really large topics that we grapple with together when we are face-to-face.

Horizon, Strategy, Practices, Habits. Lessons that have flowed down and through generations of teachers and students now land with us, as chapters for us to contemplate as we look at some of the most extraordinary headlines of our lifetimes . . . maybe in a few generations' worth of headlines. These important lessons in this book have landed just in the nick of time for those of us who hope to make sense of the world that might just be changing faster than we can grapple with on our own. Thank you, Norma, for allowing us "in the room" as we make our way through the slipstream of life.

Preface

Taj James, Nā'ālehu Anthony, and other folks encouraged me to write a book for close to two years before I came around to their understanding of why. Truth be told, Taj led the effort. A quieter dialogue with Nā'ālehu would follow each of Taj's extended, albeit friendly, oral arguments. The pilina—the interwoven relationship of our current and future work, ancestral labor, and descendants' hopes—informed and landed the decision.

At first, the notion of writing because there is an urgent need to be conversing with a larger audience was close to abhorrent. I come from a long line of teachers whose tools of experience and apprenticeship were supplemented by oft-repeated stories, practices, and the full spectrum of oral traditions. This pretty much required the sphere of teaching influence to be within sight, within reach, within the distance of hearing and following and feeling. We are modestly good at it. It works. Moreover, we believe depth requires the rigor of the face-to-face engagement and the activation of all of our senses.

What does it mean to believe and practice in a particular way and to know it is not enough for the purpose one is practicing? Well, that is a central question of these times and this book, in any case. (Insert wry chuckle here.)

And so I leaped into their faith that something offered in the tangible realm of the written word will be received in the intangible spaces of sincere inquiry by persons I have not yet met and will likely never be with. Across timespace . . . it is a leap.

A preface is generally read before the text is read but written after the text is written. It is a mini historical account and therefore a bit of context. This preface is written in the same manner as the text: a concentrate to which your own water should be added. Unlike deep sea diving, this inquiry benefits from coming up for air from time to time. You may even be disoriented by the words strung together seemingly making sense for which no logic can be made. It is part of the secret sauce of navigating the in-between spaces as you move from the one worldview that you and I intimately know yet are no longer served by, and at first observe and then slip into an emergent worldview.

Writing this book helped me understand the timeplace I choose to occupy—seeing and living in, pondering and making decisions as if this is the place and now is the time for the juncture between a devolving world and an emergent world. Inviting many to do the same increases the potential of a smoother and more fruitful transition. And so as I write these words—knowing you will read them—I am at peace with the decision to say to Taj and Nāʻālehu and other beloved provocateurs . . . yes.

Me ka haʻahaʻa, with humility, I wish you useful reading.

Norma Ryūkō Kawelokū Wong Roshi

When
No
Thing
Works

Chapter 1

Predicate

On August 7, 2022, Vice President Kamala Harris cast the twenty-sixth tie-breaking vote in the US Senate, the most in modern history. Upon leaving the chamber after sixteen hours of intense debate through amendments known as a vote-a-rama—death and life through a thousand cuts, those who voted aye cheered, cried, celebrated, and said it is a start, and those who voted nay harrumphed, declared the victory Pyrrhic, touted the ways they thwarted a full win, and said it is not the end. Within the ayes, the discipline of hewing to a win meant bittersweet swallowing, so vast it seemed between one perspective and another, though all of the same party. Within the nays, the discipline of not a single vote straying into the aye depended on hardened resolve to cast political victory in opposition, even though there were measures within the bill that some had worked years for, nonetheless voting nay, all of the same party. In a few days it would be the other chamber's task to lift the measure across the finish line—again on a straight party vote and again with the tug of war of too much and too little, in condemnation and cheering. Hard fought with multiple resuscitations over eighteen months or so, the win was so surprising that the *Washington Post*'s editorial board opined, "Green shoots of governability poke through a scorched political landscape."

In just a year's time, the green shoots of governability would seem a far distant fairytale as the US House of Representatives descended into weeks of self-inflicted chaos with the majority party too easily overthrowing their leader and by virtue of enmity's math being able to elect their own new leader. If any group of people is too precariously positioned and has only-just-enough, then that group of people must be fiercely intertwined and united in purpose and directionality. Or the minority faction of the slim majority will easily tip the balance, and the opposing party of the majority will have inordinate sway in the course of events without having to do much except to be intertwined and united in purpose and directionality.

Lest we chalk this all up to the brokenness of a specific political institution, we need only scan the headlines of the daily news feed for many examples of oppositional fights grinding to a draw. Protracted warfare in deadly stalemate. Climate activists and climate deniers in turn freezing, sweltering, and swept away in floods that are proximately caused by human choices—or is it all nature's disaster? Lake Mead disappearing and all of Massachusetts in a drought, while Kentucky floods beyond meteorological prediction. A national norm built on judicial precedent falls away on the basis of a last straw tumbling—*Dobbs v. Jackson* collapsing *Roe v. Wade*, all *v.* as it turns out. Houselessness blooms where economies are thriving. Inflation and recession at the same time—once believed near impossible by economists, though perhaps easier to accept than the growth of gross poverty in the shadow of gross wealth.

Indeed, institutions of all kinds are having difficulty being institutions. By their nature, institutions need to be steadily fed and maintained. The pandemic interrupted everything, creating a domino effect across supply chains, quarantines, and the precipitous collapse of every constituency, customer base, and market. Any weakness, any flaw, any overextension or fatigue line in the fabric or core of an institution preceding March 2020—the proximate US national pandemic shutdown—became even more so, and indeed continues to cleave.

This structural strain and near-collapse can be found everywhere. In government—local, national, international; business—small and large; organizations—longtime mainstream and newly formed scrappy; for profit and nonprofit. Utility systems struggling to factor in the cost of shutdowns and disruptions due to extreme weather conditions. Emergency responders exhausted from continuous streams of emergencies, which, by definition, normalizes extremis.

And have we talked about the weather? (Fill in here your favorite apocalyptic weather scenario that is happening every week and becomes more extreme from one birthday to the next.) In September 2022, Charleston, South Carolina, had the wettest twenty-four hours in more than eighty years and counted itself very lucky to have been spared the destruction of its neighbors to the south who, twenty-four hours earlier, suffered through twelve-foot storm surges of Hurricane Ian in one in five hundred and one in a thousand-year events that will take months if not years to recover from.

Peoples of the land, scientists, naturalists, farmers, gardeners, and pet owners have long observed the impact of climate on animals, plants, and bugs. A few animals, plants, and bugs proliferate, some mutate, and others abnormally migrate. As oceans have warmed, lobsters are no longer prolific off Massachusetts, surging in Maine as they sought colder territory, and are predicted to move even farther north into Nova Scotia. Algae bloom, plants adapt, stunt, weather-assisted bugs invade and kill off centuries-old trees. Animals lose habitat, become more susceptible to parasites and disease, mutate, and generally become cranky.

So why don't we recognize that our humanness is impacted and impaired by climate change? Not only by environmental conditions requiring resistance or adaptation, but our very beingness? Have you noticed humans—speaking for myself—more frequently lethargic, restless, anxious, defensive, and just plain cranky? An irony of human existence is that our advanced reasoning power gives us the ability to create and deny at the same moment. When there are extreme stressors, the cycle of create and deny, create and deny, can powerfully disorient.

Cranky, disoriented . . . why wouldn't we opt into our own versions of reality? Whoa!

Now there are many terrifying examples of delusional behaviors, many of which have played out in mirrored opposition. The "Awake Not Woke" (to quote a recent Conservative Political Action Conference banner) angrily denounce the stealing of elections by Libs who are brainwashing children with false history, all denied by the Woke frustrated with the paralysis of institutions to defend and advance social justice let alone fair and safe access of Americans to vote and be counted. The Awake and the Woke disdain the staidness of the middle conservative and the middle liberal (respectively), and nevertheless choices are made one by one by one, in record high ways and record low ways . . . mostly to a draw.

Yes, there are many terrifying examples. And there are a few entertaining ones. The French scientist Étienne Klein, of all people, exercised his platform in an unexpected way. As the world marveled at the first awe-inspiring and beautiful images from the James Webb Space Telescope, he tweeted a new image of the star Proxima Centauri with congratulations. Only it wasn't. Instead, Klein's star was an awe-inspiring and beautiful image of a slice of the sausage chorizo. He was joking and said so just a day or two after, but few laughed because they were inclined to believe and didn't like being laughed at. Some scientists were infuriated. People don't believe science to begin with, and now you, Étienne, have shown us to be tricky liars laughing at the gullibility of non-scientists (and a few of us, too, who recognized neither chorizo nor Proxima Centauri).

In another sausage phenomenon, a "salami-slicing attack" or "salami fraud" is the name given to a cybercriminal strategy of stealing money a small "slice" at a time so that there's no noticeable difference in overall size. There is something about this larcenous tactic that fits the times. If you steal a little at a time—a few dollars, a half-truth, some ballot boxes, swap out a few blocks of affordable homes, a bit of this and that—maybe no one will notice enough to arise and soon it will be a legitimate phenomenon and given its own name.

Whew! All of this and much, much more data of falling apartness, especially for those who are immersed in the practices of social media. I am not, and so I stand—or crouch—in the median strip and observe the roil of emotion, the jerkiness of decisions, and the maddening tiny steps by the most radical and good-hearted of beings. There is a maddening amount of falling apartness in the universe—so much so that even the intrepid are daunted, attached to the pain and to our plans, and just overwhelmed by the urgency of defense.

This I observe as I stand—or crouch—in the median strip of applied spirituality. In transformational work, it is the crisis that opens the way for big leaps. When things are going relatively well there is no need to question, and not enough energy to force the momentum of inconvenient stretches. As ironic as it may seem, it is hopeful for humankind that everything feels and looks like a jumble at the edge of a precipice. Perhaps now we will act more abundantly than salami-slicing attackers.

And from this threshold, the biggest of leaps.

> What
> To make of falling apartness?
> What
> To do
> To feel
> To have
> Too many wants
> I'm afraid
> In this falling apartness
> A hollowing out
> Of what we thought
> Believed
> Hoped
> So amazingly from all sides
> The Right

And
The Left
All sides unexpectedly
Caught beyond guard
Rails falling
In this apartness
All sides!
Ah
Some thing stirs
In this one possibility
The rising
As in yeast
Dormant
Until spit upon
With a bit of sugar and warm water
Something stirs
When no thing
Absolutely
No thing
Works
Something stirs
If
And only if
We see what cannot be seen
And hear what cannot be heard
A stance unfolds
A threshold appears
What?!

Chapter 2

Lens

On January 6, 2021, the country called the United States of America nearly fell. What we do about this, matters.

Oh my. Where are my manners?

Aloha kākou! ʻO Norma Ryūkō Kawelokū Wong koʻu inoa. Ua hānau ʻia au ma Kalihi mauka ma Oʻahu nei. Noho wau maʻaneʻi i kēia manawa. Aloha everyone! My name is Norma Ryūkō Kawelokū Wong. I was born in Kalihi near the mountains, on the island of Oʻahu. And it is here that I now live.

As a person of timeplace, more Indigenous than not, it is unthinkable to meet people—even in written form—without first introducing oneself. How else may you know how to be in relationship to what it is I am offering? The eyes we see with, the ears we hear with, are neither neutral nor generic. Of course, neither are our thoughts or words.

It would be bad cultural form to just begin without appropriate relational orientation. This is a picture of my lens so that you may orient words and thoughts in your own timeplace.

The few words beginning with aloha are in ʻōlelo Hawaiʻi, the language of the native people of these islands, the Native

Hawaiians. It is a matter of deep respect for ancestors and audience to begin an introduction so formally. I am of the generation who politically fought for language revitalization because it had reached a sorrowful nadir. In the 1980s we were down to fewer than eight thousand native speakers. Now we are over forty thousand, half under the age of eighteen. I am not a native speaker and, alas, have no facileness for language learning. Instead, the sound of the words in mele and oli (songs and chants) and the spoken word are music, balm, nourishment. The living energy of ʻōlelo Hawaiʻi is connective tissue to who it is I am, we are, interrupting the long tale of erasure by mostly white people upon mostly brown people.

As you may deduce from my name, I am of mixed ancestry. Native Hawaiian—where most of my political work has resided—and Chinese. Specifically, the Hakka—stubborn and sturdy nomads of the place called China, who retained their own language, foods, and ways across vast timeplace, refusing to be fully assimilated in the one Han culture. They came to the islands as contract workers in plantations owned by white people and stayed to grow families in relationship with the Native Hawaiians with whom they shared deep love of food, land, family, and the arc of ancestors and descendants. They also shared their love and respect of the ocean, upon which the Chinese traveled and fished, and upon which the Native Hawaiians traveled by sailing canoes without instrumentation to become the first people of these islands sometime around the year 400.

Ryūkō is neither Hawaiian nor Hakka. Ryūkō is my priest name, received when ordained in 2000 as a Rinzai Zen priest, marking a time in which my focus shifted from the ways and means of change afforded in political action, and toward the ways and means of agency afforded in transformation. A translative context for *ryu* is "dynamic energy" and *ko* is "radiating light." One doesn't suddenly become something because of a name . . . at least in spirit paths. A name is given by a teacher[1] in recognition of who it is you are and are becoming, whether you know it or not, and as an in-plain-sight reminder to oneself. In this regard, becoming a priest was about placing the internal work as that which people would externally "see." In some ways, ironically, I am a better political strategist as a thought partner now that I am free from the attachment of being an operator. A maturing kind of thing. White hairs are essential.

Kawelokū is a name given to me as a makana, a gift, upon my sixtieth birthday, by two younger kanaka—native people—whom I have come to know in the privilege of working on contemporary issues of importance across generations. They have taught me a great deal. As for the meaning of the name . . . still emerging, as a rock from beneath the ground.

Here I am, in my home. At least for the last sixteen hundred years. And in this region of the world—the vast Pacific—from the time of known human existence. This place and the peoples of this place over time—the self-sufficient and confident native people who defied extermination and continue to arise, the seafarers, the missionaries, the laborers and craftsmen and families who did not return to China, Japan, the Philippines, Portugal, Korea when their contracts were done, the refugees of war from Southeast Asia, the climate refugees from the sea-level-hugging islands of the Pacific, the land developers, the military and their families who come and go, the people who choose to continue to visit not only because of the islands' beauty and lifestyle but also because this is the least American-like place in America—shape who it is I am and how I view the world. Lenses count.

From a categorization viewpoint, it would have been sufficient to describe myself as an Indigenous woman of mixed ancestry in her mid-sixties, lifelong resident of Hawai'i, active early in life in policy and politics, particularly as it relates to Native Hawaiians, and focusing for the last twenty years on applied Zen. That would mean something to me, but would it mean something to you, enough for you to have an experience of lens? Probably not. Just as you would have much more insight if the next hundred pages or so traversed the more interesting stories of this short life and the learned stories of related and unrelated ancestors. Tempting, but we are in an urgent slipstream. The shorter versions of a hand-ful of stories are likely to find their way into the unfolding text. How else may we be in relationship with each other, so critical in this digital existence that drives to all matter of transaction—choices, judgments, acquisitions, and discards.

The lenses with which we view and act into the world, among other things, form our perspectives—our points of view. My teacher, Tanouye Tenshin Rotaishi, sometimes answered the question of "What is the truth?" with this: "The truth is the inter-section of everyone's perspective, if we could only know that." We can't. His point was to show the architecture and the slipperiness of righteously judging what is true or not, and instead to prac-tice reflective discernment, remembering one's own perspective is what it is we see through our own lens. What are the lenses of at least two others in vicinity of this truth? Just one other is one short of **tri**angulation.

Prescriptively, there is first the recognition of lens—its pres-ence and its specific characteristics. Second, the interruption of one's own lens to remove the habit filter otherwise known as our bias. Third, an understanding of how another person's lens pop-ulates their perspective, hearing it without our own judgment, and therefore catching a glimpse of what is behind, underneath, desperately wishing to be known, and a preview of what may come. It is listening without filter plug-ins.

In the treble of these times, it is impossible to talk about per-spectives and lenses and hearing and seeing things with clarity, even in complexity, without talking about and warning about the magnifying hair-on-fire effect of social media. Here I open a door that I have observed without direct experience. From my laptop, never my flip phone, I tend to email and scan news on a small handful of sites (across ideology while avoiding immersion in the farsides). Tech sales folks are quickly repelled from the delusion of selling me anything when I casually open my flip phone. My Instagram account is managed by others and hasn't sent anything out in oh about three years. The Facebook page for Norma Wong is literally another Norma Wong. Really—somebody else; not me. TikTok and Twitter (now known as X)? Forget about it. With these caveats, it would not be revolutionary to observe that socialized media has the digitally enhanced capacity to keep people in the comfort and stimulus of their own perspectives, an echo chamber of their own worldview. Social media is a steroid. And like any drug, the immersive lens of social media inflates our loves and our grievances.

Dial it back, dial it back. Dial it back.

Here, in a quieter place—though never silent. In the knowing of one's perspective without defense or magnification. From this vantage, hear and see and feel and ultimately begin to understand what is going on and what is not. Listening and observing, assembling the intersection of worldviews in the same timeplace, and determining . . . toward what end?

We often need the assistance of spacetime to help us see and hear and feel in this way—for some time to have passed, and some space to grow from the tightness of our overwhelm. (And yes, we'll explore both spacetime and timeplace more as we go along.)

Spacetime does not heal all things. Spacetime can provide a means to learn from even the nearness of history, and the possibility of triangulation.

On January 6, 2021, the country called the United States of America nearly fell. A gift of the congressional hearings is the amount of experiential data they have provided, allowing for a

DIY IMAX, a complex reconstruction from the perspectives of individuals, groups, perpetrators, defenders, emotions, energies. The hearings are not neutral. There is an investigative goal, and an intent by the committee's stewards that the United States will not fall. Like many, I watched all of this play out in real time on January 6. And yet, this multiple-faceted replay, with some time in between each, has immeasurably added to our and my understanding of the how and why and what of that moment, as well as the explosive energy into every moment and place thereafter, some of which we are seeing and some of which has yet to manifest. It is urgent and invaluable triangulation.

What we do with this, matters.

Maka'ala! Ho'olohe! I ka wā ma mua, ka wā ma hope. Eyes wide open! Listen carefully! The timeplace of the past, that which it was, the timeplace of the future, that which it will be.

Chapter 3

Slipstream

There is a lot going on in the world. So much so that it feels like we are being pulled and pushed along, and the next moment, falling far behind. The energy and directional forces are change-inducing elements, in and of themselves. Having some understanding of the science of what it is we are feeling is useful in figuring out what to do in it and about it, how to take advantage of the gusty flow and, in effect, being purposefully in the slipstream.

According to *Wikipedia*, "A slipstream is a region behind a moving object in which a wake of fluid is moving at velocities comparable to that of the moving object, relative to the ambient fluid through which the object is moving. The term slipstream also applies to the similar region adjacent to an object with a fluid moving around it."

Physicists talk about time as being more about relationships than constancy. Or at least that's how a nonscientist may interpret what a physicist is saying in one of those articles in which a scientist patiently explains to a layperson the mysterious wonder of the universe. Time+place, or shorthanded timeplace, is how we experience the course of events in time and in place, across time and across places. When more things happen in a human-made measurable period of time, that feels like everything is speeding up and time itself is moving faster. Entirely inaccurate from the point of view of simple math, but not unheard of in the advanced algorithms of the continuously changing variableness of physics. We don't need to understand the physics to have the felt experience.

In *Finding Nemo*, the protagonist's father, Marlin, rides Crush the sea turtle on the fast-moving stream of the East Australian Current. Clocking in at about 4.4 miles per hour, this current isn't even the fastest, believed to be the Gulf Stream, at 5.6 miles per hour. An Olympic swimmer can match this speed on a short sprint like the fifty-meter (0.03-mile) freestyle. In comparison, the cast of *Finding Nemo* could have, if they wished, traversed twelve thousand miles at the same speed as Michael Phelps, jetting along with far fewer flapping of fins.

The amazing aspect of ocean currents is that they exist above and below of, side by side with, the variable and slower movements of oceans. A vessel upon the ocean's surface will be propelled or slowed down or directionally thwarted because of currents of energy miles wide, miles deep, and hundreds or thousands of miles long. The phenomenon is a vast force of nature, studied and utilized by mariners for thousands of years.

There is a lot going on in the world. While I sit on the floor typing these words to the tunes of HAPA, cat sleeping just out of sight, slight breeze visible in the leaves of the neighbor's tree, one eye occasionally landing on the clock to make sure that I'm not late for my meeting . . . while I do these things, the personal bubble of timeplace moves deliberately apace in four-by-four time and I am swimming with easy strokes in shallow water toward shore, buoyed by the tide. At the same time, immeasurably gigan-tanormous stuff is happening all over the world—bustling, creating, growing, dying, inventing, destroying, monotonous burger flipping, raving, icebergs cleaving, drones targeting, some quiet scurrying through dark forest floors but mostly cacophonous pontification. More than ninety-five million Instagrams are sent each day. Though a single person can only view about 150 or so in that time, the impact of the millions roils on. 95M × 95M time.

There is a lot going on in the world, and it feels like even more is being stuffed into each moment. Urgently pushed or runaway momentum? Impact-wise, it doesn't matter. We are in a swiftly moving current much of which has been created by humans and human actions over time and space. This phenomenon is short-handedly called *collective acceleration.*

To be clear, it is a made-up term—no scholarship, or science. (Although there is an electrical engineering term so named, there is no derivation to be made.) Collective acceleration is the short-handed description of the felt experience of living in the world during a time in which everything seems to be "going faster" so much so that it is better captured as "much more going much faster." So many people in so many places across cultures, nationalities, social and economic circumstances, societal roles, ages, genders, and ideologies are in the felt whirl of this acceleration that we can confidently say: this is collective phenomena. Not all, of course, but enough to say: **we** feel this, **we** are dealing with this, **we** are affected by this. Not all, of course. The human emerging from a four-by-four rhythm cocoon of just a few weeks will likely be astonished by the storms that arrived and dissipated, the businesses that are merging or calling it quits, the deals made or fallen through, the laws overturned, the voices newly legitimized. Slipping out of the current doesn't mean the current stops. Indeed, upon reentry, the point we left is now far downstream.

To be clear, this is far from the first collective acceleration moment in human history. These pivotal, cleaving moments are the proximate cause of one or more environmental, human conflict, human aspiration, technological, or economic upheavals or events.

Here we briefly talk about four upheaval-event categories: large-scale epidemics and pandemics, mass migrations, wars, and technological advances.

There have been many world-changing epidemics and pandemics. The Antonine Plague, AD 165–180, took five million lives. The Plague of Justinian, likely the bubonic plague, hit the Byzantine Empire, 541–549, claiming 10 percent of the world's population. Fifty percent of Europe's population were lost during the Black Death, caused by *Yersinia pestis*, 1346–1353. Viral hemorrhagic fever, the Cocoliztli Epidemic, took fifteen million lives in Mexico and Central America in the sixteenth century. During the same century, 90 percent of the Indigenous population of the Americas succumbed to a combination of illnesses imported by Europeans. In comparison, the COVID-19 pandemic has taken an estimated three million lives so far, about 4 percent of the world's population.

Epidemics and pandemics. Massive disrupters of families, communities, health systems, the trajectories and the demise of entire peoples, altered immune systems that are passed to succeeding generations. Rapid decline of the labor force both disrupts and shifts economies including, mostly temporarily, the balance of power between those who labor and those who require labor. Inventions arise, especially in medicines, public health practices and ways. The institutions of the time—family, community, government, businesses, fraternal organizations, religious centers—arise to the need or fail to do so, each learning in the process and acting or reacting in temporary or permanent ways.

In the past, there have been numerous mass migrations. The ancestors of Polynesians—the many peoples of the islands of the Pacific—migrated from the coastal areas of south Asia around 1600 BC, 3,600 years ago. Polynesians continued to migrate, ending in populating Hawai'i in AD 400. Among the largest forced migrations through capture, kidnapping, and slavery relocated between ten and twelve million people of the sub-Sahara to the Americas in the span of 360 years. Construction of the Three Gorges Dam in China, and related flooding, displaced 1.2 million people. The Potato Famine, 1.5 million. Nearly all of the Indigenous peoples in the lower forty-eight United States were forcibly relocated—forced internal migration. Their lands were largely occupied by European migrants, along with other parts of the Americas, parts of Africa and Australia, totaling about sixty million European migrants over four hundred years beginning in the 1600s. In current times, tens of thousands have fled the violence, unsustainable climate conditions, and poverty of Central America.

Migrations occur as people move away from and move toward. Moving away from sustained flooding, sustained droughts, violence and conflicts, overcrowded conditions, diminishing possibilities, and, in recent years, rising seas. Moving toward possibilities, safety, jobs, promises. Others are stolen, coerced, forced, driven out. If this were a political analysis, there would be a distinction between immigrants, migrants, refugees, and asylum seekers, and forced labor. Migrations change the course of the places people came from, and the places people traverse to. The size and time compression of mass migrations mean the impacts are identifiable and measurable and specific to those peoples, those times, those places. The dislocation of Indigenous peoples robbed subsequent generations of place-based wisdom. Migrants contribute to peoples and places. Migrations in and of themselves are sharp pivots. "That" used to be our life and future. Now "this" is our life and future, known and unknown.

There were and are the many wars. How many have there been? It is apparently easier to measure the amount of time when there were none. Defining war as a conflict that claims a thousand or more lives, Will and Ariel Durant in their *Lessons of History* (1968) estimated that only 8 percent of human history (which they conservatively measured as the past 3,400 years, a more Western perspective of civilization, editorially speaking) has been without war. We tend to see the armed conflicts that are in the news. Can you guess how many conflicts claimed over a thousand lives in 2021–2022? Sixteen armed conflicts claimed over a thousand lives, two of which have claimed over ten thousand lives (Myanmar civil war and Russo-Ukrainian War). Can you name at least half of these conflicts? Chances, no. No war ends wars.

The many wars disrupt and displace. They uniformly destroy place, both human-made and environmentally born. Wars perversely destroy economies while supercharging industrial complexes, simultaneously feeding jobs while displacing livelihoods. Health care usually improves post-conflict because of wartime learnings, but these improvements mostly accrue to countries with intact infrastructure and the means to adopt and distribute.

Wars divert and devour resources: humans, money, raw materials, intellectual capital, goodwill.

The technology discoveries of one era become the floor of what's possible and define the aspirations of a society, and sometimes a generation and a civilization. Without the discovery of boats some ten thousand years ago, fishing would have remained a subsistence practice, trade limited to regional bartering, and human migration, well, not a thing. The invention of papermaking in the second century marked the beginning of large-scale and portable knowledge transfer and communication uncoupled from oral history and human memory. Arguably, the Industrial Revolution would not have been possible without the discovery and harnessing of electricity—powered by whatever means, not only to power industry but also to power the discovery of other technologies. About 65 percent of the world's population are too young to know a world without the all-pervasive internet, and it will be close to zero in a mere fifty years. But 37 percent of the world's population don't use the internet, mostly due to access issues defined by poverty and proximity to infrastructure, which in turn impact access to information and basic services that are increasingly only available through internet-related technology. The triggering of the immune system within our own bodies with a replicable protein would not have been possible without the technological breakthrough of mRNA, which is estimated to have prevented between ten and fourteen million deaths from COVID-19.

As these few examples show, technology has had a profound and frequently "sudden" impact on the trajectory of human events since the beginning of human events.

And here we are.

Here we are in the convergence of global environmental phenomena, collapsing economies, mass migration.

Warming oceans, disappearing lakes, stronger hurricanes, droughts, wildfires, floods, the demise of species. Insolvent governments, the thinning fortunes of the global middle class, gross wealth accruing to an elite few, sharp decline of global extreme poverty, steady increase in the ranks of the working poor, labor shortages, stretched supply lines. The hardening and collapse of national borders as countries struggle to manage refugees, asylum seekers, migrants that don't quite meet one legal category or another but nonetheless are fleeing the collapse and chaos of their home states, a steadily increasing stream with sudden surges fueled by wars.

Whew!

If you google the phrase "may you live in interesting times," among the subjects that will pop up is "what are some curse words in Chinese." There are also claims that the phrase "may you live in interesting times," thought to be ancient Chinese in origin, is really a modern Western notion. Without going down a rabbit hole (with apologies to rabbits), consider that the Chinese word for "crisis" includes the word 机. 机 is part of the word for "opportunity," but by itself is more accurately described as *a critical juncture when and where change begins*. Contextually, the ancient wisdom of this is that there can be no big leaps without risk and the presence of the unknown.

This accelerating time of convergence is a time in which crisis is omnipresent. The collapse of all things feels imminent. We feel it because it is impossible for there to be such turmoil on the ground and in the universe itself without great waves of energy, or perhaps the energy is created by the internal turmoil **we** feel. Both are probably true, which magnifies the signature and momentum of this great current moving through the timeplace.

On August 8, 2023, Hurricane Dora tracked south of the Hawaiian Islands, bringing strong gusts of wind and very little rain. A series of wildfires erupted in drought-stricken pockets, and calamitous fires clocked at a mile per minute consumed the town of Lahaina. Too many lives lost. Homes destroyed. Thousands displaced. The land now holds nearly unbearable pain. In this placetime of tragedy, what can be said about possibility? And yet, before the ash had settled, humanity immediately arose in self-organized pods to provide food, supplies, clothes, comfort, aloha for neighbors and those-we-have-only-recently-met, well before and with more ingenuity than the overwhelmed governments. People from across the islands and indeed many places beyond focused their attention on supporting those who were supporting many. Within a few months, the bubbling up of critical questions and ideas on how to not return to the flaws and fractures of pre-wildfire Maui unsettles the established power dynamic and heralds, perhaps, a new way forward. A consuming fire is both a tragedy and a critical juncture for change that will inspire many. If the juncture is ignored or swept aside, if we step away rather than step in, then it is only a disastrous tragedy.

Thus, seen and felt, herein lies 机, the critical juncture for entering the pathway of the current. 机 is the threshold between the chaos of collective acceleration and entering the slipstream. While we may hesitate, not knowing many things, it is the unknown that holds the most powerful possibilities. So take a breath. Take a step.

Chapter 4

Threshold

机
Opens the door
And from this threshold
A horizon beckons
Should we walk forward
Or not?
Heads down
In the chaos of the moment
How can we see what lies ahead
Or around the bend?
Not seeing

Not hearing
Not feeling
The timeplace yet to be
The threshold, a gate closed
Heads down
Caught
In the moment's endless chaos
Endless urgencies
Urgent suffering
(And the ego of our response)
机
It's self unseen, unheard, unfelt
This timeplace
Within
Threshold a locked gate
Bound in anxiety's foggy
Shroud
Entangled
And yet
All we need
Here
Feet on ground
Raise our gaze to the horizon
Breathe again
Breathe again
Breathe again
All we need
Here
Alone cast adrift
In spiraling search

One other
1 + 1
More than
"+" a powerful "and"
(The Sufi know)
Two others
1 + 1 + 1
A stable stool
For others to sit upon
Suddenly more
Becoming
We
A human threshold
Arising beyond
Individuality's false promise
Isolating power
Starts with one
Gains possibility with two
Launches
Beyond
At three
A sturdy platform
For others to join
Themselves
Just one and one and one
A human threshold
Arising beyond
Breaking bread
Sipping tea
Steaming rice

Sharing stories
At fits and starts
Perhaps
Remembering
Beyond the deafening clamor of human demands
Beyond and within
Hollowed out
Now filled
With
Stories shared
Rice steamed
Tea sipped
Bread broken
Revealing
Tastes differ
Hunger shared
Thirst is thirst
This thing
This human thing
Connection desired
Even in grievance
We seek
Affirmation
So
Why not
In possibility?
Why not?
First
Lift our gaze to the horizon
Walk there, walk there, walk there

Each step a leap
Across the threshold
The juncture
Where change
Begins
机

Chapter 5

Horizon

机 is where change begins because the juncture is so critical it creates the impetus for change. However, change can take many directions and ways. At the timeplace when we finally look up, gaze on the horizon, which horizon will we see, which horizon will we move toward?

As in any journey, this most consequential one requires our knowing where it is we are going.

Let's start with the mundanely consequential. Leaving the house on an errand, what are we hoping to find? The "what" generally defines the "where." The "where" raises the question of route—the "how" to get there. And traffic and road conditions are factors in which route we choose to take. We also measure our choices based on the amount of available time.

(Most of us know in our bones how to successfully navigate errands and nonetheless flounder on the strategy of other things. Muscle building . . . for another story, perhaps.)

Horizon is a what, a place, and a time.

It is the "Not seeing / Not hearing / Not feeling / The time-place yet to be" that keeps us mired in place. Easily resolved! Let us see! Let us hear. Let us feel.

At the 2022 convention of the Council for Native Hawaiian Advancement, a panel of mayors of the four counties of Hawai'i were asked about the future of tourism, a complicated and emotional issue for native peoples. When it came to Kaua'i Mayor Derek Kawakami's turn, he told the story of his future self. Now retired, he is taking his grandchild (yet unborn . . . hint, hint, son) to his favorite beach (unnamed here to interrupt unhelpful geo-tagging) to pass on his love for riding a few waves. They pulled into the lot and easily found a parking spot. (Here the audience burst into appreciative cheers and clapped at the novelty of this twist.) On the way to the shore, they pass the island guests who are picking up rubbish as part of their kuleana (mutual responsibility) as guests, and the guides who are greeting newly arrived guests with "Hello, aloha. Here is sweet-smelling biodegradable sunscreen that won't kill off the coral reef. Oh, thank you for bringing your own. Swim on this side please."

His ending pause was met with more appreciative cheers and, needless to say, it was difficult for the other mayors to follow with their well-thought-out but nonetheless blah blah policy talk.

The mayor's future story is only twenty or so years in the future. A near horizon, indeed. And yet, a simple story allowed us to see, hear, and feel all that we needed to know about which horizon we desire and will work toward. The blah blah policies of regenerative tourism, ecologically safe products, community stewardship were brought to mutually thriving life. The story is all the more appealing because other horizons loom large. Enforcement officers ticketing locals and tourists for mounting infractions. Locals driven away from overused shorelines. Rubbish left for someone else to pick up, or not. Not wanting to kill the economic engine. Mounting tension between those who want this and those who want that, mostly locals with insinuations of outsiders.

We have tendencies to see, hear, and feel the future as a simple trend line. When we are pessimistic, the horizon is murky, dark, and every doomsday prediction comes true. When we are optimistic, the horizon is crowded with the many things we are optimistic about. If "this" or "that" is the horizon we see, hear, and feel, then "this" or "that" is the horizon that will come true. Our choices and our actions will carry out our predispositions, including the ones we dread.

Instead of a predestined trend line, think of and experience the future as the living story that descendants live in, in which they describe how ancestors imagined it and then made it true.

Creation requires just that—both the imagining, and the hard work of making it true.

(In between the imagining and the hard work is strategy . . . for another writing.)

Where do we start?

As a person in his vigorous mid-forties, Mayor Kawakami looked to his retired self, one or more grandchildren in tow. As a person in the mid-sixties, I look to the time just before passing—perhaps as a much older person—and the time after I have passed but people who knew me are still traversing their lives. Younger folk tend to look to the unimaginable time—when they are middle-aged. This is the near horizon.

As a person who is exercising the muscle of future storytelling, though a novice compared to distant ancestors, I reach out to the timeplace of seven generations hence, in the vicinity of 140 years to come. This is the far horizon, or at least the farthest that the practice of a seven generations arc may hold.

Between the near horizon and the far horizon, there will be a tipping point in which the circumstances and the data will tell the story that the world emerging in the far horizon is inevitable, provided hard work and good choices continue.

The story in the near horizon is almost always rooted in problem-solving (unmanaged tourism) and hope-filled thinking (my son will have a daughter and a son). The leap isn't far, but it is still a leap. Otherwise, why would a convention hall full of native people applaud in happy surprise for easy parking at the beach? The scenes of the story are clear and sequential. I took my grand-child to my favorite surfing spot and pulled into the nearest stall.

In the near horizon, details count and are about doingness, and the rough calculation of how many units of doingness one may accomplish between now and the descriptive picture of the near horizon. A twentysomething aspires to be an organic farmer supplying yummy and nourishing produce to urban families ("near horizon") and thinks about the kind of land, the where of land, the how much it will cost of land, the kind of crops, the synergy of crops, winning the battle of bugs and disease, and finally how to get the heirloom potatoes, the swamp spinach, the oyster mushrooms, the bittermelon, the beautiful edible nasturtiums to the tables of families who will enjoy and be fed and break the monopoly of agribusiness ("the many details of doingness").

Whether in the realm of the near or the far, the interaction of people and institutions other than me-myself-I and the small we . . . the interactions matter. Who will agree with what it is I see and desire? Join? Resist? Cooperate? Support? What are the other ideas in the same timespace? Will these ideas compete? Magnify? Detract? Will the conditions and circumstances of timeplace be conducive? Lift and buoy? Overrun and sublimate? In the near horizon, we will have distinct opinions—supported by data, or not. In the far horizon, vast currents of interactions will amass, roil, and stall in our imagination or the projections of futurists (a.k.a. their imagination).

Near or far, our fear, or doubt, or suspicion of the what-ifs can stall our forward movement, keep us in a wishful suspended animation or circular and ever more detailed and yet unsatisfactory process of inquiry. Unhelpful! And yet, this is part of the baggage of the human condition. Processing is an acceptable, cautious way to be productive. (Ouch.) Sometimes, the best we are able to do is to simplify process. If you are nurtured, comforted, and become more powerful with process, you are likely to be repelled by many ideas in this writing. There is a timeplace for process. And a timeplace for silent reflection. And a timeplace for action. And a timeplace for resting.

So far, we have traversed the more familiar ground of the near horizon—the story and mechanisms of the timeplace within reach if we are motivated enough to lift our eyes to the hills, to the timeplace of cities so far away they are small specks, beyond the shore to where the ocean or lake meets the sky. It is too far to walk or swim, and yet within sight.

What do we make of the far horizon? Well. If we were in a room together, I'd offer to tell you a story of a timeplace at or just beyond the tipping point, by definition a big leap or three beyond the near horizon, within sight of the far horizon. We would take a break beforehand, allowing for visits to facilities and the coffee bar, the stretch and inevitable even if discouraged text message check. The future story has its own rhythm, and no unfolding thing may be rushed nor interrupted without losing its essence and energy. My story practice is to reflect, breathe, reflect, pause, and allow the story to unfold along the lines of narrative without processing or notes. That is my practice.

Lacking the in-the-room moment, we turn to stream of thought in written form. Here it is, as best as may be.[3] After the offering, we'll come back into the thought partnership of what it may all mean.

Here it is, as best as may be.

Here we are. The descendants of peoples who met in January of that year in the 2020s when the world felt both promising and fraught. Yaht! Holomua! Mmmmmmmmmmmm (humming) . . . Every few years from that time hence, we the descendants have gathered until we are the kupuna, the elders, and descendants again and kupuna again, repeating the cycle and passing the baton of kuleana (mutual responsibility), with ancestors at our core, guarding our backs. Here we are. Eight generations, 160 years hence.

Before we gather again, we enticed our cousins from the many corners to celebrate the special makahiki, the time of remembrance, gratitude, renewal, and reset. We have much to reflect upon. And so our cousins came. Several from Turtle Island, Alkebulan, the aboriginals of The Land Belonging To No One, Oaxaca, Cymru, and the Ryukyu Islands. Folks who now reside on and steward the islands of Polynesia and near-Asia, the Mediterranean, and in sight of many continents. The scientists who rebirthed in the embrace of ancient wisdom informing the future void. The futurum physicist who plainly said he's coming for the food. Farmers and fishermen bearing simple bounty, fresh and preserved. And a good number of monks of various paths— for the music and easy company of fellow travelers. Shhh. Don't tell. There are a handful of governance leaders. We will embrace them with anonymity and familial care. We have their backs as they have ours.

Here we are on the lands of the peoples who first sang "*O ke ehu kakahiaka* . . ."[4] those many generations past. The red dawn of our people became the red dawn of many peoples. 机

In a season's time we will meet with many others. Our ranks will swell. The hui of many hui, the group of many groups. There are whispered stories of a solemn ask to be brought forward by governance leaders. On the lee side of the great repurposing of military institutions and ambitions, there is the question and doingness of waging peace. There are whispered stories we will be asked to lead the many ways and means, to form and teach the corps, to herald the cause farther and wider. It has taken us many generations to arrive at this juncture, and the governance leaders instinctually know how important it is to move the waging of peace farther and wider than the laws of the many countries, beyond the dismantling, in the interspace and mycelium of human structures and ways. This will be solemn, generational kuleana for the hui of many hui. If the whispered stories come to be.

So this makahiki is consequential. On the precipice again, meeting the red dawn. We are here in the pre-makahiki potluck, sprawled over the expanse of lands where deep beneath us the life-giving water was first poisoned with jet fuel so extensively it threatened existence of all life on Oʻahu, now cleaned in entirety, the fuel-soaked hardened soil, the aquifer's permeable rock holding the water, and the water itself—heavy lifting over two generations, defying conventional wisdom, technological limits, and political convenience. Many beyond this place gathered support for this national effort and, in turn, were inspired to bring back from death the life-giving waters of their places.

Next week we will visit the stewards of the low-lying areas reclaimed from the sea level fall, nearing a three-decade phenomenon after sea level crest. No one can know how far the seas will fruitfully recede, though scientists and culturalists across disciplines are endeavoring to penetrate the question—is this a balancing moment or the beginning of a hundred-year planetary change? While they measure and argue and ponder, the stewards of the low-lying areas are developing the story of the near horizon and begin laying out requisite ecological and human habitation strategies of the near horizon story.

I'm sorry . . . you want to know what it is we are eating today? Well. Several days, in the tradition of these things. The three days to gather and prepare and eat as we are doing so, the day to feast and sing and dance and play music and tell stories, the day or two to clean up and eat in thanks for those who prepared and cleaned up, including the distribution of foods in the surrounding communities. Two dozen kinds of poke from deep sea and near shore fish now abundant since seasonal and area periods of resting from fishing has several generations of fruition, with cultivated limu (seaweed), pa'akai (sea salt traditionally harvested), and some poke prepared controversially with dried wild berries. (Though not a fan, I respect palate choices.) All manner of dried, stewed, roasted, and barbecued meats of many land, air, ocean, and lake animals. Cultivated and wild rice, steamed in al fresco glory, gently stewed, porridged, and paella style. Breads baked on site. Pa'i 'ai (hand-pounded cooked taro) prepared on site. Hand-pulled noodles from the hand-pulled noodles competition. Bittermelon with black bean sauce from a recipe passed fourteen generations, mouth to watering mouth. Artisanal tofu. Heaps of vegetables, many too sweet and crispy or pleasantly bitter or brightly citrus to spoil by cooking. And potato salad. (Note: macaroni salad in odd years; potato salad in even years.) Here we sit and feast and sing on the bluff, five hundred feet above the human-made caverns that used to house a vast and secret fuel storage facility no longer, overlooking the harbor where the United States entered a world war, though now holding vessels for uses other than conflict including the storied Polynesian deep ocean sailing canoe fleets, and the lochs of prized Wai Momi oysters once grown solely to clean the waters and now internationally sought for eating, preferably grilled with a little juicy sauce. Whew!

Here we are. (Long pause.)

Though this narrative comprises about half of a future far horizon story delivered orally, it should be sufficient to illustrate the ways and lessons of the far horizon.

Chapter 6

Worldview

Here we are.

Though the narrative in the previous chapter comprises about half of a future far horizon story delivered orally, it should be sufficient to illustrate the ways and lessons of the far horizon.

First and foremost, the far horizon story is always beyond the apocalyptic time when everything completely fell apart and the skies were dark for so long no one knew lightness nor blueness.

Huh?! What?! Wait! How can it possibly be that the far horizon story is always beyond the apocalyptic time? You've obviously been inhaling da kine . . . k k k. S-t-o-p. Take a breath. Exhale long and slow. Please . . . Before you discard this way, listen for a moment as to why, how it works, and why it matters.

The far horizon story is the embodiment of everything we hope our descendants will live into. It is the product, the destination, and the time made possible by hard choices, consequential decisions, big leaps. It is beyond the sightline of knowing only if we work toward this timeplace inch by inch as we fiercely search the ground for clues. It is entirely within the embrace of glorious possibility when we lift our gaze and tell its story.

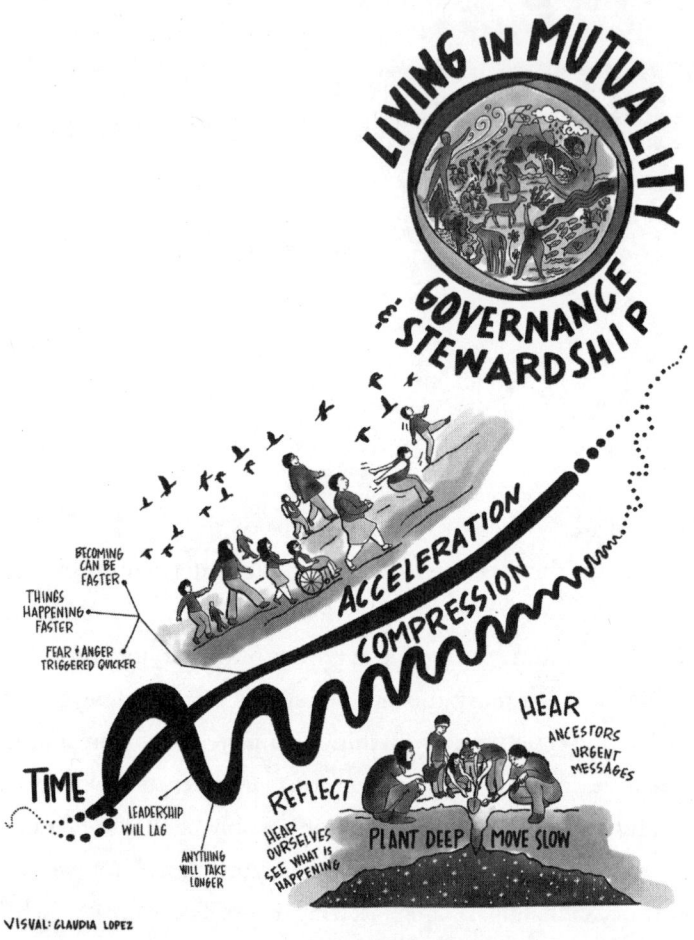

LIVING IN MUTUALITY GOVERNANCE & STEWARDSHIP

ACCELERATION

COMPRESSION

BECOMING CAN BE FASTER

THINGS HAPPENING FASTER

FEAR & ANGER TRIGGERED QUICKER

TIME

LEADERSHIP WILL LAG

ANYTHING WILL TAKE LONGER

REFLECT

HEAR OURSELVES SEE WHAT IS HAPPENING

PLANT DEEP | MOVE SLOW

HEAR

ANCESTORS URGENT MESSAGES

VISUAL: CLAUDIA LOPEZ

Do not worry. The apocalyptic timeplace will occur. Some may even observe—I be one, as you may have surmised—this current timeplace is drifting haphazardly in the riptide of collapse. The story of the apocalyptic timeplace is merely a dramatic extrapolation of the now. Only in hindsight, in the timeplace several generations downstream, will we be able to definitively say whether this current moment and place is in the beginning or the near middle of total collapse or, fantastically, beyond the crest. The trajectory of collapse, how dark it will be, the grimness of suffering, what may be possible on the other side . . . much of that story is dependent upon whether Earth and her beings commit and act into a worldview of fruitful thriving as illustrated in a future story.

We know the story of the collapse—or at least it is vivid in our imagination. We have much less imagination of the timeplace on the other side. What we cannot imagine is more difficult to create. And what cannot be created cannot become so. Thus, the far horizon story should always take place beyond the apocalyptic time when everything completely fell apart and the skies were dark for so long no one knew lightness nor blueness. It is there and then we need to practice into.

Besides the geotemporal, there is the ball of wonderment—the values, the ways, the spirit mechanisms defining the world as we would have it be.

A fact exists not in and of itself but as a data point in a field of what it is we believe and therefore know to be true. The confusion and clash of the current collectively accelerating mash is defined by the litigation of facts and alternative facts. (Though many derisively snorted at this term coined by Kellyanne Conway, she was nonetheless accurate.) It is possible to have alternative facts if there is a schism of beliefs and the underlying values of those beliefs. If we believe that certain people—by class, gender, race, ethnicity, age, ability, education, profession, societal role, nationality, geographic place of birth, ancestry, religion, political affiliation, ideological spectrum—are better, more legitimate, more right, more prized, more coveted, more holy, then, by definition, other people are worse, not as legitimate, more wrong than right, less prized, not coveted, less holy. Who would you look to for the facts, what is true and what is not? Who would you discount and disbelieve?

A fact exists not in and of itself but as a data point in a field of what it is we believe. The field is a field, a tapestry, a bowl of stew, a story of many chapters that come from a cohesive collection of stories—not a single data point. The data point is evidence, a tiny window into an entire world. The interpretation of the relevance of the data point and the subsequent story of the string of data points furthers our understanding of a world, one that may intersect with or entirely diverge from the worldview of another person.

Tens of thousands more folks, double digit percentages worth, register and show up for an election, much more so than can be accounted for in the normal fluctuations of electoral cycles—say those that monitor and report such things, and even more than expected by those who have been organizing to make it happen. Record-breaking. The actual number is raw data. The characterizations—"more than can be accounted for; more than expected"—are stated by us as facts. The reasons for the surge are quickly gathered in our individual and collective thoughts faster than research may formulate questions let alone measure. That doesn't matter much, as our declaratory thoughts burn bright, land hard, and are echoed back to us, thus meaning more and trusted more than any research. Who are those guys, those pollsters and researchers and analysts, anyway and how come they didn't ask *this* question of *these* people?! Our individual reasons register as facts—as real as any raw data. So much so that the data point may morph, and be repeated, and held as the truth in its magnified or distorted or minimized form. And then we act upon all of it. There is no ordinary way, and therefore it must be an unlawful way, for the numbers of voters to increase so quickly. And—reaching back into our preconceptions of how these things happen—*they* must be stopped from upsetting the normal, the regular, the lawful course of things. Close the loopholes in the law. Now. No no no. You call it closing the loopholes but what you are doing is suppressing, oppressing, discriminating against. We will fight you. Raise lots of money. The fight is won because the fight was lost.

And yet, the lines stretch around blocks. More records fall. In spite of the best efforts to not allow that to happen, and beyond the best efforts to overcome the new rules designed to not allow that to happen. Energy moving in a particular direction can have its own momentum, gathering people one by one, and then more and more, until the critical mass is its own force. It is a phe-nomenon of one of the trajectories in a collectively accelerating worldview—one that has in its fervent aspiration "the world as we would have it be."

The values, the ways, the spirit mechanisms defining the world as we would have it be matter. The pause to take a breath and lift our eyes to the horizon, the mountain-scape, beyond the edge of the desert or ocean, is to tell a story that is beyond the moment's fierce fights and to say—in story—the manifestations of the values, the ways, the spirit mechanisms of the world as we would have it be.

Can you name the ways from my story? I am curious what it is you would say. Perhaps you could put a piece of paper across the rest of this page, hiding what it is that is said, and say what you would say. Then take a peek . . .

... Multigenerational continuity of values and responsibility ...
Worldwide relationships based on deep work and community ...
Indigenous peoples who have thrived and work beyond their
ancestral birthplaces, which are recognized by traditional place
names once thought erased ... A strong purpose of world peace
that must be worked for and is the responsibility of the spiritual
and common folk ... Governance beyond the institutions of government ... Reclaimed land and elements of the land, especially
water, in mutual relationship ... Stewardship ... Looking and
planning forward, w-a-y forward ... Beyond food security, food
abundance and sharing and remembrance ... more!

If your appetite is whetted in a good way, I caution you to
stay as long as may be possible in the stories themselves and the
descriptors of values and ways. Yes, there are frames in which all of
these may fit. Interdependence. Mutual governance. Multigenerational stewardship. Restorative ecosystems. Restorative healing.
To name a few. And yet, even naming the few, here, surely you can
feel the difference in the energy and therefore the possibility more
so in two dozen kinds of poke from deep sea and near shore fish
now abundant, enjoyed by spirit leaders and scientists and farmers from across the globe, in relationship based on deep work and
community, pondering what will unfold stepping into the fierce
struggle for sustainable peace.

Almost certainly you will see, hear, and feel other values,
ways, and mechanisms in the story than the ones named here. Or
naming these formations, you would tell a different story or a sister
chapter in the same story, taking place with other descendants in
a timeplace on the other side of the world, perhaps. "Meanwhile,
in the new growth of the Amazon basin, no longer desolate clear-
cut swaths of rutted tracks ..." "The children of the one hundred

boroughs of the land of the Lenape brought seeds and seedlings, new book chapters to share, favorite snacks, birdsong recordings to weave into the decadal one-hundred-hour song composing marathon . . ." If a horizon story—near or far—has resonance beyond its principal storyteller, it is because it has strong underpinnings in which many stories may be told, many peoples find themselves in, innumerable scenes of work in progress.

This is the emergent worldview. Aspire to nothing less so.

Chapter 7

Leap

How do we aspire and live into the emergent worldview, the nothing-less-so timeplace that feels enticingly beyond our reach?

Eyes on the horizon. Heart's core tethered to Mother Earth as she connects to the entirety of the universe. Breath low and slow. Consciousness permeable to the full spectrum of spacetime. Flexible and purposefully ready, just leap.

There is embodied preparation and worldview pivots that set the foundation for leaping. Of course, the exercise of strategy, casting back from the story of the thriving future, and building the just-enough infrastructure to support a critical mass of intrepids.

And no leap occurs without leaving the safety of what you know and leaning into a constantly changing unknown. Thus, it can be said that leaping is transformative evolution in which there is evolving transformation.

Leaping takes courage, faith, and appetite. Courage is not an absence of fear; rather, it is what we are about in the face of fear and doubt. Courage is "stuff," frequently quiet, rarely bravado.

Courage is needed to consequentially leap because there are known and unknown risks. Only the foolish have no fear, the Taoist strategist Sun Tzu opined, lamenting at the plentitude of fools. Faith is what we have when we believe in ourselves and what it is we are about, the tangibility of our horizon story (not the probability). We have faith in our fellow travelers, fellow warriors, fellow poets, fellow farmers, fellow cooks on the path we are building together because we are building together. Trust undergirds faith. Or is it the other way around? And if there is no appetite, no desire, no magnetic pull toward that which needs to be done, must be done, then the excitement will be short-lived. Appetite makes perseverance possible, that internal resolve to weather the most confusing and chaotic days without losing our way and ways.

Thus, it can be said that our beingness both precedes and permeates our doingness. (There is, indeed, doingness. Leaping isn't worth much as a wishful kind of thing.)

My most enthusiastic colleagues habitually accord to this order: Leap! Act! Aim! Allow me to make a case for a consequential shuffling:

- Leap (in our mind, heart, core)!

- Aim (as in strategically and tactically align and orient within and toward the emergent worldview)!

- Act (in a leaping way, discarding the habit of incremental steps, toward that which we aim)!

Redundantly reinforcing—the first leap is indeed one of beingness. And it is closely associated with what and where we are leaping toward. We are more likely to imagine and strategize into an expansive possibility if we first leap in our mind, heart, and core, while interrupting the habit of not committing, not desiring before we know all the details. Without the initial leap, our imagination can be limited to the boundaries of our current possibilities. This facing squarely and leaning into becoming without a hairsbreadth interval of hesitation . . . this is the becoming part of beingness.

A

Frog

Prima

Ballerina

Mighty

Flea

Flying

Squirrel

Excited

Child

We

Are

Becoming

What

Where

Why

We

Leap

Toward

Thriving

Yes

Please

Thriving

Chapter 8

Habits

If our future story is one of productive thriving and *if* our desire is strong to move toward thriving, then why don't we make the decisions and take the actions to *go there now*?

There is, sadly, a long list of reasons, so justifiable that we could end this slim book right here, right now. If that were so, the chapter should be renamed "The Reasons for the Status Quo." Instead, 机 beckons at least a reframe that may open a door. May I offer? Instead of reasoned reasons, consider reasons arising to habits.

Habits are unconscious repetitive acts. As humans, we have many. Physical habits. Individual habits. Family habits. Cultural habits. Societal habits. Gendered habits. Generational habits. Organizational habits. Occupational habits. Regional habits. National identity habits. Ideological habits. Species habits. Habits accrue because, over time, they work for us, feed a need, attach to our well-being even if they don't work for us. We tend to think of some habits as "good" and some habits as "bad." From the perspective of making leaps into the slipstream of collective thriving, there are no good or bad habits. Just habits. By its definition the "thing" that is unconscious cannot be consciously summoned or interrupted. In its consciousness, the pattern can be seen for what it is. Choices made. Courses turned. Pivots made. The child in us leaps.

A whole book might be written on habits. This isn't it. Instead, our focus is on the habits that keep us in a state of observation, hesitation, desiring without leaping.

The habit called process: A deeply seated and learned habit of grownups is process. Process is simply the series of articulated actions or steps taken to move from "here" to "there," to achieve a particular end. Having process, knowing process, practicing process are ways for us to have order and certainty, even before we start. Process can be institutions unto themselves. We may default to process in an endless and circuitous doingness to seek order and certainty with many steps before a genuine first step. While creation is a process, there are many ways in which the habit of process keeps us from creating. As a habit, process fills the space with things to do, things to say that are often rehearsed or pro forma. Okay . . . enough about process.

The habit called consensus: The definition of consensus is "general agreement" . . . which is interesting, because that isn't the habit known as consensus. In its habit form, consensus arises and hardens to the necessity of committed alignment, often at the level of weeds; therefore, difficult to achieve in a fractious environment of mostly individualized power. Further, the habit form of consensus requires committed alignment before decision-making and actions. As a locked gate, all decisions and actions become the process to achieve approval to move. Whoa! Double whammy!

The habit called not leaving anyone behind: As a beneficial though perhaps misguided binary to everyone acting for themselves, the value of not leaving anyone behind can morph into a habit of not moving until *everyone* is ready and willing to move. It is extraordinarily difficult to achieve a total state of readiness and willingness. And, thus, this habit preordains we will not move.

The habit of performance as a limiting factor: The dark side and omnipresence of performance measurements, performance-based assessments, institutionalized feedback, outcome-based education, and the like is that we begin to conform our behaviors to external measurements of success, goodness, disapproval, and failure. These are excellent tools for control, productivity, and achievement. Shockingly, they rarely build an internal muscle for endeavoring beyond stated expectations and previous experiences of approvals. A habit of performance can produce pro forma.

The habit of external affirmation: Perhaps the habit of performance comes from a habitual need for external affirmation, or perhaps our need for external affirmation is nurtured by the habit of performance. In any case, leaping into the unknown, by definition, isn't possible if you are waiting for external affirmation to do so, or to acclaim and reward you upon leaping.

The habit of underestimation: We tend to underestimate how much we are capable of, how much courage we have or may need, how much experience we already have. In an endless cycle of figuring out how much more "right stuffness" we need, we feel ill-equipped and unworthy of consequential pursuits. We underestimate how much time and effort will be required, especially for complex tasks. This sets up a paradox of expending a lot of effort only to arrive unprepared. We habitually underestimate or undervalue the energy and impact of desires and passions, hopes and dreams, all emotional adjectives and emotional states. This is a strange habit of not accounting for the human element and expecting logic's facts to compel and propel. Included in the rubric of underestimation of overestimation, which is an underestimation of how we overestimate.

The habit of short-term thinking: The habit of being too near a horizon creates a timespace that limits both time and territory. We are nonetheless drawn to it because we can see it, or at least believe we can see it. It is within our grasp, and therefore it is real. This limits our possibilities, and we are rewarded by the success of small incremental gains.

Habits are unconscious repetitive acts. Shining a light is a first step to recognizing the patterns of habits, their predictable and well-worn paths. Raised to a level of consciousness offers the possibility of choice, as in I choose to be in this pattern and consciously make it work for me, or I choose to interrupt this pattern and consciously take a different path. Both choices offer possibilities. Only interruptions offer propulsion.

Chapter 9

Practices

If all unconscious repetitive acts are habits and patterns of habits, how does one cultivate so-called "good habits" without them becoming habits? By practicing. Facile. Finito.

Huh?! One more time, please.

Practices are **conscious** repetitive acts, acts taken **consciously** to "perform (an activity) or exercise (a skill) repeatedly or regularly in order to *improve or maintain one's proficiency*" (from *Oxford Dictionaries* online; italics are mine).

In practice, not so simple. In life, never-ending. And yet, satisfying.[5]

Brushing one's teeth as a practice—in ways that pay attention to the otherwise untended—improves one's dental health, day by day. Securing one's glasses in places where they can be readily found, no matter where you happen to be, is one less aggravation. Leaving each place better than when you arrived cleans and transforms in a totally doable way.

Iterative improvement is a function and by-product of practice. With discipline, the outcomes are even more satisfying. In consciousness, patterns can be seen for what they are. Choices made. Courses turned. Pivots made. The child in us leaps.

Practices are all about interruption + cultivation. Interruption of habits (named in the previous chapter) + cultivation of ways and muscles for choices, horizons, and pivots. Here are the fabulously fundamental five:

The practice of clearing the deck(s): To go deep, or to go far, to go deep and far, one requires a light(er) load to facilitate travel. Most of us, especially the diligent, enthusiastic, socially conscious, north of moderately responsible, urgently motivated "us," are trafficking in too many things in too many places for too many reasons. We are the amateur not-ready-for-the-circus jugglers, dropping many balls and plates and fire swords yet tantalized by the possibility, nonetheless. To go deep and far in the slipstream of this collectively accelerated 机 requires the fullness of energy and attention. A cluttered deck, holding too many things, allows energy to dissipate and attention slide. Doing a lot distributed among many things means doing a little about many things ≠ significant impact. Clearing the decks is a practice of choices—as in making actual choices, rather than having many glittering choices that are too full of possibility to make any. Not making choices is a choice, albeit one that paradoxically leaves one in a state of fewer and fewer true choices.

The practice of breathing: If a leap is only in one's mind, the many things that need doing, and undoing, will not happen. A leap is an embodied movement. Great height, great force, quick movement. In paradox, a leap into great things requires us to be grounded. To know in the entirety of our being that "this is it!" It is a hyper prefrontal cortex activity and, therefore, requires us to be in grounded breath, low in the body, and in rhythm slower in its exhalation. A meditative breath is between 3 to 5 cycles (one inhale + one exhale = 1 cycle) per minute. A grounded breath never exceeds 10 cycles per minute except in physical duress and then for measured periods of time. Long-term shallow breathing can leave us feeling foggy and muddled. Long-term fast and shallow breathing activates our amygdala and fight-flight reflex, which loops us back to even faster and shallower breathing to defend the amygdala presence. Knowing these things helps not an iota. Only the daily practice of conscious breathing cultivates the mind-body and, yes, the mind-body-spirit for 机 work. Breath is fundamental.

The practice of climbing and standing on the hill: We have many feelings, beliefs, and perceptions as we traverse the fields of work and play. We are collectors and dispersers of facts as we see them, facts as we know them, facts as we interpret. We are immersed in the fields we traverse, most of which are thick and weedy, or cluttered with land mines, or generously occupied with glittering objects. From the perspective of the fields, it is difficult to see a horizon, let alone other players, movements, obstructions, dangerous curves, lurking opportunities. We need to climb and stand on a hill to get a longer, wider, 360-degree view of the field of play. Some who read this might say, well, that was an unhelpful metaphor. Standing on a hill won't help me. Well, unless you have literally experienced standing on a hill, you won't know when it is important to untangle yourself from what you are in the muddle with, and how to exercise the inquiry to gain the hill's perspective. Go stand on a hill, or at least a table. "I can't see what's happening." "I don't know what's going to happen." "When will this begin?" "When will this end?" "Where is that coming from?" These are some of the sensory indications that it takes more than time to reset. Come back into grounded breathing. Clear the decks. Exercise your curiosity and gather images and data points. Seek the views of others who are standing on hills. Suspend analyses and conclusions until you have a many-sided view of things, just as you would if you were actually standing on a hill. If truly a practice, this isn't a reset. It is what is periodically practiced in order for the "greater" perspective to be the ever-present view plain. For shorthand, I sometimes say: "eyes on the horizon."

The practice of cultivation: There is a bit of farmer practice, gathering practice, beehive practice useful to preparing to leap, and to keep leaping. This is especially so if you are pivoting from doing this work as an individual to working in the commons with the commons. Among the most critical cultivation practices is the cultivation of relationship. I say these words as a certified introvert. Networking isn't included in the definition of this practice and, practically speaking, networking can't come close to the beingness of relationship. The emergent worldview is built on the strongest and most flexible of intertangled relationships in which we daily practice interdependence, a way in which each person is important to every other person for collective existence and thriving. This is a distant and impossible ideal unless we have a practice of cultivating relationships. "Cultivating" is practice in itself.

Tending, feeding, weeding. Codependency is not interdependence. As codependents, we lean upon each other's strengths, weaknesses, tendencies. In interdependence, we are each as whole and as strong as we can be at any given moment, and yet choose to be intertwined. In relationship, the 1 + 1 is often > 2. Three in intertwined relationship become the foundation (think: a stool) and the core of a critical mass. Tending, feeding, weeding.

The practice of storytelling: To create something, anything, you need to envision it. "Vision" conjures words and concepts. A concept still needs a drawing. A drawing begs for a prototype. To create into the emergent worldview is about re-imagining how a whole world would work, why that would be so, what would be happening and what would not, and how it would become so. You could traverse the route of vision, concepts and values, and story as the living experience of the vision . . . or you could start with story, and find embedded within the concepts and values for which strategies would need to be built and implemented in order for the story and the many stories to become so. In any case, there is the practice of storytelling, a nearly indispensable piece of the puzzle that unlocks our barriers and expands our capacity. Storytelling is an early muscle that may have gone flabby over the years. As children, we wondered about many things in our wandering, and "made up" stories to answer each and every thing that we wondered about. We did that. Naturally. Wonderfully (as far as every doting adult was concerned). Some of us stopped wondering, so there were no stories to be told. Some of us wondered and looked to others for answers or began to believe that there are no answers. Or we got lazy and googled it. Or believed that only children tell stories. Well . . . we need the children with us, now. Exercise that flabby muscle! Interrupt the editing toward perfection! Just practice.

Facile. Finito. Choose one. Begin.

Chapter 10

Strategy

Running pell-mell toward the horizon of our desire has a romantic appeal. No more may be required if the horizon of our desire is no more than tens of yards, perhaps a favorite shave ice stand just across a not-too-busy parking lot, about 76 degrees mostly sunny skies, winds out of the northeast at 10 miles per hour. The just-go-do-it strategy is among the most frequent (and only marginally successful) strategies in all human history.

Or alternatively, we may deploy a long exercise of figuring-out-and-second-guessing-strategy-like process, in committee, inching along or seemingly reversing course, leading with rhetoric as an energy shield against actual movement.

These are instinctual, uncalculating habit patterns that keep us out of the slipstream. Especially in the circumstance of choosing to interrupt the tethers that keep us bound to the shakiest of status quos, strategy becomes a practice of interruption.

While most of us are not strategists, the simple bones of strategy are in (nearly) everyone.

Need to go to the store. Come upon an unexpected traffic jam. Look around to see what may be happening. It is so slow that everyone stops for long intervals. Better save gas. Turn off the engine until I need it; turn on; turn off.

Need to go to the store. Come upon an unexpected traffic jam. Look around to see what may be happening. Perhaps check a news feed. Begin to plot in your mind, or use one of those apps for alternate routes. Try the next right that loops back in about half a mile.

Need to go to the store in the next day or two. Come upon an unexpected traffic jam. Let's do this tomorrow.

Need to go to the store in the next day or two. What other errands can I do at the same time? Come upon an unexpected traffic jam. Well, the third thing on the to do list is in the direction that looks free and clear. Let's go there first.

Surveying provisions in the cupboard and fridge, making a list to go to the store in the next few days. Sister calls. Need anything? Where are you? Yes, please. Tofu, yogurt, and eggs. Thus, adding three more days before entering the "need to go to the store in the next day or two" zone.

There are at least another half dozen alternative strategy scenarios, but you get the point. Alternatives. A fundamental bone of strategy is choice, and choice does not exist without alternatives. Alternatives shrink when you are right upon whatever it is you must do. The scarcity created in too little time and too much urgency narrows the field of alternatives. In the other direction, alternatives unhelpfully multiply without ballast or direction when you don't know where it is you are going, when you're going, whether you should go or not. Alternatives are glittery objects and rubbish on the floor without the prefrontal cortex function of good choices. But there are no choices to be made if we are unable to see, feel, hear, understand the variation of possibilities before us, out on that horizon and down there all around you as you stand on the mountain. No strategy is possible if we are mired in weeds and mud, or chasing the emotive pull of our amygdala, or especially if we do not know the answer to **why**, otherwise known as **purpose**.

If our meta purpose is to make the leap beyond this fraught moment in order to implement into a world that thrives, then at the very least we need a word (or a small set of words no sturdier than a sentence fragment) that captures the intent and energy of this meta purpose. If it is to be one word, I choose "thriving." If it is to be a small set of words no sturdier than a sentence fragment, I choose "interdependent thriving."[6] "Interdependent thriving" describes and answers the question of: Why do I do what I do? I do what I do to move ever closer to a world that lives in interdependent thriving. Or what is my meta purpose? My meta purpose is to actualize a world of interdependent thriving. And how will I measure success? Success will be measured by my descendants[7] experiencing interdependent thriving in actuality and as their operational worldview.

The purpose of interdependent thriving aligns with an emergent worldview that leaps beyond the tightly bound fight-to-the-draw of the current moment. It is worthy of the work, the struggle, the celebration.

There are many other purposes that align with the horizon of fruitful emergence, the horizon we may indeed call interdependent thriving. Wellness. Enough food. Technology as servant. An Earth that is healing and heals. Diversity, a defining and divine strength. Uniting and reflective spiritual health. Governance in mutuality. Peacemaking. Responsible freedom. Enoughness. Wholeness. Gratitude leads. Respect rules. Bees and butterflies are back. No one wants or needs a gun. Wisdom earns wisdom.

Each of these purposes sits in a horizon of possibilities, images, conditions, habits interrupted, and practices . . . well, practiced. A horizon of fruitful emergence can be cluttered. A focal point on the horizon is a constellation of intended outcomes, a fruitful cluster rather than a clustered cluster. A focused constellation serves as a magnetic pull for direction and effort, and the alignment of strategies.

With a clear and magnetic purpose constellation, strategies are not just action plans and operational processes. Strategies are the ways and means to "get closer" to our intended horizon.

"Getting closer" can take a while. The way in which we proceed, the what we are promoting and deciding upon, the why we are acting . . . all count toward the cohesion and possibility of a horizon of fruitful emergence. Strategy ways and navigational methods that are not consistent with the values of a horizon of fruitful emergence impede our evolutionary progress.

What are useful strategy ways that work with the slipstream?

Transitions that leverage and meta morph: When we aspire to leaps, our ability to do so and to have others leap with us may be . . . more aspirational than possible in the moment. It is useful to employ the strategy of transitional steps that exercise the muscles necessary to take on the fullness of leaps. The leap from activism to governance, for example, benefits from the intermediate practices of decision-making, resource responsibility, human responsibility, and seeing down the road that has twists and turns.

Relational: Strategies require understanding, buy-in, standing aside, energy, and execution. These are human endeavors and, therefore, no strategy moves from paper to action without humans speaking to other humans.[8] The art of strategic communication begins with relationship, not with messaging. We need people—who are specific even if they are many—to understand, to buy in, to stand aside, to bring their energy, and to execute. The fruitful horizon has many relational characteristics. We get there through relational practices and strategies.

Creation: Strategy as it pertains to the fruitful horizon must provide the space, the time, the invitation to create and to be creative. The fruitful horizon is not an iteration or a cut-and-paste or a save-and-resurrect.

Capacity: Strategies need to take into account the limited, gasping capacity felt by most people and institutions. There is no leap to be made when burdened. We cannot become if overcome. The magic of capacity is that when we choose-to-do-a-few rather than choose-to-do-more, our capacity increases and has air to breathe. A strategy may need to be extraordinarily discerning in how it differentiates the amount, the distance, the intensity of any given action as it is implemented across many individuals and institutions.

Truth and response storytelling: The strategic narrative tells the story (not the analysis) of what's going on, why and how things are happening, what's desired in a compelling and inclusive way, and shows the ways to get there. This is a story of invitation, participation, and belonging that sits in honest and humble truth, thus interrupting the strident and righteous truth. Truth and response storytelling is the shareable blueprint of a strategic trajectory.

And trajectories? Well. They're pathways that are all about navigation. The straight-through-the-opposition-no-matter-what is always available and, parenthetically, among the least successful strategic practices. Instead, consider:

Come with: Inviting folks to join in and be a part of is the spirit of the "come with" navigational practices. This is more than an allyship. It has the flavor and feel of a well-organized potluck in which fun and work are shared. The beginning stages of a "come with" practice will feel like a burden if held by a host. If it remains at that formation, then this is more of a "will carry you" practice, which is not sustainable.

Flow around: There will be obstacles. Perhaps the gatekeeper stands in your way. Or the person who seems to be oppositional to anything new, or anything so-and-so favors they will be opposed to. Or institutional rules tightly circumscribing conduct, presenting it as a boulder in the stream or perhaps even a dam. (Sometimes, we are our own obstacles.) We can always take a stand and fight to change the mind of the obstinately opposing person or thing, but the assessment must be made: is this fight the end goal, or is there merit and juice in moving beyond the obstacle to act and create beyond the wall? Instead of spending many hours unable to achieve consensus let alone consent, are there eager folks, ready and willing to move? Consider flowing around the boulder(s), especially the ones of your own making.

Burrow under: Burrowing under is a version of flowing around. Sometimes, the breadth of the open fight is too fierce or dangerous to flow around. Flowing around happens in plain sight. What burrowing under feels and looks like is engaging in work that furthers our forward movement out of sight and out of mind and out of the way of the people and institutions that are obstacles, and thus make our way beyond the spacetime of entrenchment.

Waiting for the tide: Sometimes we need high tide to float our boat. Sometimes we need low tide to scrape barnacles off the hull. As we seed ideas and possibilities, it takes time for people and energies and desires to amass sufficient quantities and qualities for there to be "groupness." This is a waiting for the rising tide. Sometimes we need to regroup or engage in purposeful resting and restocking. This cannot happen during the high tide and so we must seek the conditions to be in a low tide.

There are many embedded values in the horizon of fruitful emergence. And there are certain values that embed the most fruitful of strategies consonant with a horizon of fruitful emergence.

The value of extended kinship: If I, if you, if they, are in kinship relationship to me, to you, to them, then our work and our struggles take on different behavioral possibilities. That isn't to say that kinship relationships are without difficulties and animosities and even violence. It is to say that when there are such behaviors among family, we hold those as less than ideal, abnormal, out of balance, and lacking love, trust, and accountability. Our expectations differ when there is no value of extended kinship and there is/are instead my family, my friends, my community, and your family, your friends, and your community with which we may have allyship or respect or tolerance or estrangement or disgust.

The value that the world is an island: Having lived the entirety of my life on an island that is among islands for several generations, I experience the literal closeness of cause-effect, come-go, push-pull. A large-scale event in one place quickly impacts the entirety of the island, even before it is chronicled in the news. If the pandemic taught us anything, let it be this—the entirety of the world is but an island. When Lahaina burns, we all grieve. Technology accelerates impacts and cannot be put back into its magic bottle. Thus hold the value of our closeness. Operate and strategize as if it is so.

The value of "art is long, life is short": This saying by Hippocrates is the favorite quote of the late composer Ryūichi Sakamoto. No matter how long we may live, it is short in the scheme of humankind. Therefore, value life and its possibilities. Make the most of it. Take leaps. Pivot toward and away from. If we are artful in how we live and decide and act, then that which we fruitfully create will reverberate long after our one life.

This is what it would mean to live the strategy of a good ancestor.

Chapter 11

Choose

Ultimately, the strategy way of a good ancestor is about choice. If it were only that simple.

In the individualistic, it's-about-my-rights, materialistic ways of the modern era, merely making a choice does not equate to moving in any specific direction except toward one's desire or belief at the moment of the choice. Choose not to take a vaccine. Choose an abortion. Choose to AR-15. Choose to love. Choose to ignore. Choose to hate. Choose abstinence. Choose to be on time. Choose to not show up. Choose double fudge brownies with fresh whipped cream drizzled with salted maple caramel and roasted cacao nib sprinkles.

And the ever-favorite: choose to choose everything-every-where-all-the-time. To be clear, this is not making a choice, except in the most indulgent of worldviews of being able to have everything without choosing. And yet, it happens all too frequently. Why so? There is a temptation to judge by saying, well, it is just about being spoiled. But unfortunately, it is more complicated than just indulgence. Living a life as if there are no consequences piles up, even for those who can afford to pay to have others pick up the pieces, or countries that export consequences. Choosing everything-everywhere-all-the-time lacks awareness let alone the value of responsible relationship.

Sigh (as in Big Sigh). We long for the free, uncomplicated time when we didn't have to make any choices. This is a sign that our memories are very, very short. There has never been a time in our one biological life let alone in the life of humanity when not making choices was free and uncomplicated.

In its stead, the more choices I make the freer my life becomes.

Why is this point worth examining, and even belaboring? Because a pivot, a leap, a strategy, an embrace, any thing and any path other than the one you/we are on right now, requires consciousness and discipline of choice. Hard stop.

So, let's say we have the will to do so, and the gumption to interrupt the ways we slide into nonchoice. How do we choose?

Following the contours of "art is long, life is short," we waste no time, even throwing ourselves into the pursuit of the clutter-free path toward our fruitfully entangled future. Less zigzagging between doing things that are distracting and more doing things that are critically important. Less pondering, pondering, pondering and more take-a-breath-to-reflect-and-simply-decide. Less navel gazing and more open stance reflection. Less fussing while lost in the weeds and more decisive actions with the view plane from the foothills.

No leap, no pivot, can be made without choosing. There is the choosing to do so, and there is the choosing to interrupt whatever habit patterns are keeping us from (fill in the blank). We must interrupt the strong adherence to the known and choose into creation that which, by definition, is yet to be known. We must interrupt the habit of believing that we have no choice but do this alone and choose into the kinship of teams and community. We must interrupt short-term thinking and choose multigenerational strategies that nevertheless have many short-term benefits.

In choice, the presence and our recognition of 机 can provide both context and urgency. Nothing like a critical juncture to spur us out of inaction, to remind us that treading water is a temporary tactic of survival that is mostly designed to stay in place. 机 is the critical juncture where change is possible and, therefore, choices that are made have greater potency, more gravitas, enhanced possibilities . . . **if** we choose into it.

If.

Chapter 12

H$_u$

H$_u$ is the Human Quotient. Who we are matters.

There is a fraught reflexiveness in these times to define our-selves in some series of markers and in doing so define who it is we are not with maximum judgment. In tragedy, we identify with and identify against. In joy, we assume the who of the We. We cannot be said without Them whispered. We/Us. Them/Not Us.

Perhaps this has always been so. And yet, the folks who study these things have discovered that there were Neanderthal who loved *Homo sapiens*. So perhaps the great leaps of seeing each other beyond the markers have also always been so.

The "who we are" of the H$_u$ is much more than nationality, race, identity, or any category of demographics, or gender, or biological age, socioeconomic status, ableness, wellness, level of education, status, title, job, role, height, girth, hair length, gun ownership, or . . . politics. And it is impossible to require, insist, litigate people to see, feel, and hear beyond that essential place, the beating heart of the H$_u$.

I used to think of the H$_u$ as the bundle of characteristics and traits—some learned or honed, but most innate—that constitute the behavioral foundation for the best (and worst) leadership, warriorship, strategy, voice. Take courage, for example. Without courage, there is no appetite for risk, and no significant leap can be taken without the presence of risk.

But even before we consider what these traits and characteristics may be, it has become necessary to address the most fundamental H_u—whether we have the capacity to have and behave with humanity. To see ourselves as members of a Great and Humble Human Race. To evolve toward our better selves. To have an instinct to be in relationship to and to be kind and to accept kindness with gratitude. Each day, the newsfeed delivers more data of our near infinite capacity for inhumanity. Will the Human Quotient be hollowed out, replaced by a set of human-made rules of conduct?

It is the H_u that will determine whether we—the human race—will make it fruitfully to the other side of this fraught and fought timeplace. Whether we move from frenemy to tolerance, tolerance to acceptance, acceptance to being in relationship with, being in relationship with to mutuality, mutuality to interdependence. Yes, please, may we.

May we—yes, we—invite ourselves into the discovery and connection. We—the ready, the willing, the open . . . becoming. Too much to ask? Farther, beyond, buried deep and hidden behind the many identities, our greatest possibilities lie.

Of and with courage, that deep and faithful current that moves even in and because of the justifiable fear, gathering strength and inspiring people into their own.

Of and with clarity, so much more than glasses may afford, jewels emerging from thoughts' rubble, the bracing wind of decisiveness ever-present because.

Of and with humility, held with humor in the ethos of forever learning, pride impervious to easy bruising.

Of and with compassion, hewed from the struggle of many encounters, far beyond empathy's perch, a dew's drop or fog bank as may be discerned.

Of and with self-discipline, slayer of indulgence, keeper of health, moderator of extremes, engine of practice, friend of Mother Earth.

Of and with emergent wisdom, growing in the commons, the property of no one, beyond AI's imaginative machination, knowledge learned and pierced.

Of and with the human spirit, the energy within and beyond, a small ember meets starlight, from ancestors to far-flung descendants, cultivated and shared, never denied, with a single breath known, close to the ground yet soaring freely, fierce in possibility, the keeper of all hopes.

Chapter 13

Arise

We
The keeper of all hopes
Suspicious though we may be
Fear lurking in all the corners
Doubting our own readiness
Caught in the innumerable webs of delusion marking
This timeplace and spacetime
Spinning with seeming chaos
And yet cunningly so
By human ambition
Not the H_u's call
In our stead
The sneering white-knuckled amygdala
Of our own making
May we forgive ourselves
And move on move on
To that place of maximum possibility
机

Asserting and arising
As yeast that cannot be denied
Its potential deliciousness applied
To the stuckness
Of all things fought to a draw
Without satisfaction
We cannot linger to watch
Entertaining though it may sometimes be
Instead the urgent yearning
For a timeplace not yet built
Here
Not out there
Here
Not in the stars
For the stars have already done their best to birth
Who it is we are
This One Earth
Not yet
One Peoples
Divided
In all the ways imagined and unimaginably
Some took a breath
And discovered
It is possible to breathe
Necessarily so
If one is to gird courage
Climb into the foothills
At the time of the red dawn
To perceive the horizon
But a blur from sea level

Even as it continues to rise
It cannot buoy us
Into the foothills we must climb
That we may feel, hear, and see the
Story
Of our own telling
So vivid now that we are beyond, beyond
The pull of fractionness
And pulled instead
In the slipstream of our collective spirit
Waging peace
As our ancestors hoped we would
And descendants counted on
We arise

Notes

1 My teacher was Tanouye Tenshin Rotaishi, born Stanley Tanouye, a Nisei (second-generation Japanese American), who lived among Native Hawaiians. He was a martial artist, a public school teacher of music, a student of Omori Sogen Rotaishi, an understated and therefore influential counselor, and a teacher to many. We celebrated the twentieth anniversary of his passing in January 2023, at Daihonzan Chozen-ji, in Kalihi Valley on the island of Oʻahu, Hawaiʻi.

2 This calligraphy is the script version of the character meaning "a critical juncture when and where change begins."

3 This written story was written as stream of thought—in one sitting with very few edits—to mimic the process of narrative storytelling.

4 From the song "Kū Haʻaheo," which became the anthem of the 2019 Mauna Kea movement.

5 In Zen, the interruption of habits—which ultimately obscure our being able to be fully human beings—is brought about through practices of specific things and of the everything. Being "in-practice" is a practice in and of itself. Discipline and patience are required and cultivated. It is a never-giving-upness kind of thing, with tangible and intangible benefits. Continuous practice of the mundane and the sacred is a Zen way of living, a way of interrupting all habits accumulated from the day you were born, that your True Self may be visible and available to you.

6 Actually, it can be said that I choose "mutual aloha" as my purpose. As taught by Native Hawaiian elders and described in Hawaiʻi state law, "aloha is the essence of relationships in which each person is important to every other person for collective existence."

7   Though I have no biological descendants, I have descendants, none-
    theless. As do we all.

8   Yes, I do have a view of AI, but that is not for this book.

Photo and Illustration Credits

About the Author

Norma Ryūkō Kawelokū Wong Rōshi, familiarly known as Norma Wong or Wong Rōshi, is an emerging kupuna (elder) living in the land of her birth, Hawaiʻi. She is of Hakka and Native Hawaiian ancestry. Her ancestors lived in the Hawaiian Islands centuries before Western contact. Earlier years were spent in community and policy work, and she served as a Hawaiʻi state legislator and as a policy advisor and strategist to former Governor John Waiheʻe. The term Rōshi recognizes her responsibilities as an 86th generation Zen Master of the Rinzai Zen line. In addition to spiritual teaching, Norma has spent many years in the applied space—the direct application of Indigenous and Zen ways, values, and practices to living and transformational change critical to our times.

About North Atlantic Books

North Atlantic Books (NAB) is an independent, nonprofit publisher committed to a bold exploration of the relationships between mind, body, spirit, and nature. Founded in 1974, NAB aims to nurture a holistic view of the arts, sciences, humanities, and healing. To make a donation or to learn more about our books, authors, events, and newsletter, please visit www.northatlanticbooks.com.